PUFFIN BOOKS

THE CONKER AS HARD AS A DIAMOND

'You? Conker Champion of the Universe? Everybody else would have to play with glass conkers for you to be Conker Champion of the Universe. Remember last year?'

Alpesh certainly did remember last year. He didn't need reminding that he'd lost every single game. That's why he's on the lookout now. On the lookout for that special winning conker – the conker as hard as a diamond.

But does such a thing exist? And if so, where on earth is he going to find it? Little Alpesh's ambition leads him into the most incredible scrapes in this riotous, action-packed story.

Another book by Chris Powling

ROALD DAHL: a profile

Chris Powling

The Conker as Hard as a Diamond

Illustrated by Jon Riley

PUFFIN BOOKS

For Ellie

PUFFIN BOOKS

Published by the Penguin Group
27 Wrights Lane, London, W8 5TZ, England
Viking Penguin Inc., 40 West 23rd Street, New York, New York 10010, USA
Penguin Books Australia Ltd, Ringwood, Victoria, Australia
Penguin Books Canada Ltd, 2801 John Street, Markham, Ontario, Canada L3R 1B4
Penguin Books (NZ) Ltd, 182–190 Wairau Road, Auckland 10, New Zealand

Penguin Books Ltd, Registered Offices: Harmondsworth, Middlesex, England

First published by Kestrel Books 1984
Published in Puffin Books 1985
10 9 8 7 6 5

Made and printed in Great Britain by
Richard Clay Ltd, Bungay, Suffolk
Set in Palatino

Chapter One

Hello!

This is the story of Little Alpesh and the conker as hard as a diamond. It's rather a *strange* story. To tell you the truth I'm not sure I believe it myself – and I'm telling it. Let's hope you're better at believing things than I am.

Alpesh was a little lad with wide-awake eyes, jet-black hair and a grin on his face so big and friendly that you felt like his best mate the instant you met him. Why was he such a jumpy kid, though? Why did he keep on staring upwards and downwards and from side to side all the time as if he were looking for something?

Well, he was looking for something —
something so special nobody in the world
had ever found it before. Actually, nobody in
the world except Little Alpesh had even
thought of *looking* for it before.

What was it?

I've already told you. For weeks and
weeks and weeks now Little Alpesh had been
hoping to discover THE CONKER AS HARD
AS A DIAMOND.

'Do what?' the other kids said.

'The conker as hard as a diamond,' said
Little Alpesh, 'that's what I'm looking for. It's
got to be round here somewhere.'

'But there's no such thing,' said the other
kids. 'How could there be a conker as hard as
a diamond? Why, with a conker as hard as a
diamond you could beat anybody. You'd be
Conker Champion of the Universe.'

'Exactly,' said Little Alpesh.

'You?' said the other kids. 'Conker

Champion of the Universe? Little Alpesh?
Everybody else would have to play with
glass conkers for you to be Conker Champion
of the Universe. Remember last year?'

'Yes,' said Little Alpesh sadly.

'Last year you didn't win a single conker
game. Not one.'

'I know,' said Little Alpesh.

7

'You were *useless*. We only had to breathe on your conker and it fell to bits.'

'I remember,' said Little Alpesh. 'I was there, wasn't I?'

'*You* were,' said the other kids. 'But your conkers weren't. Or not for long, anyway. Reckon a bubble on the end of a bit of string would have had more chance than your conkers did.'

'Reckon it would,' Little Alpesh said. 'That's why this year I'm only going to play with the conker as hard as a diamond. I'll beat *everybody*. All I've got to do is find it first.'

'Good luck,' the other kids laughed.

And they took Little Alpesh off to a football match to cheer him up. You see they liked him a lot, really, and they knew it wasn't his fault he only had to pick up a conker for it to go off pop like a balloon. He just wasn't what you might call a natural conker player.

Guess what, though? All the way to the football match and all the way home afterwards Little Alpesh kept staring upwards and downwards and from side to side. Every second he was hoping to catch sight of the conker as hard as a diamond. He even had a good look round the stadium at half-time, just in case, while during the match itself the football reminded Little Alpesh of a huge leather conker.

'Concentrate on the game,' the other kids said. 'Forget the blinkin' conker season – it's the football season that's just begun. The conker season is ages away still.'

But Alpesh knew it wasn't. He realized that soon the leaves would be falling and the conker pods dropping. Everywhere kids would be choosing the best for special treatment – soaking in vinegar or baking hard in the oven or freezing in the fridge. Everyone would have a favourite trick for a favourite conker. Everyone except him, that is. For him ordinary conkers went mouldy in vinegar or split when he put them in the oven or shrivelled in the fridge. They always did. If only he could find the conker as hard as a diamond! Would it ever be his?

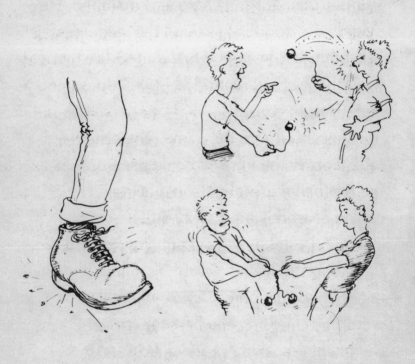

Well, the conker season came and nearly went. All over the neighbourhood kids were having contests — contests with wheelies (where you get an extra go if the conker you hit turns a complete circle on the end of its string); contests with heelies (where if the conker you hit comes off its string you're allowed to stamp on it); contests with snicker-snacker (where you try again if both strings get tangled together). Every other kid apart from Little Alpesh had at least one conker which was a twenty-er or even more (which means it had beaten twenty other conkers).

'Want a match?' they asked him.

'Not yet,' said Little Alpesh.

'Still looking for the conker as hard as a diamond?'

'Still looking,' said Little Alpesh.

'Good luck,' they always laughed.

But Little Alpesh had no luck at all. By now it was hard to find an *ordinary* conker, let alone the conker as hard as a diamond.

The big kids must have snaffled the lot, Little Alpesh decided.

Then, one Sunday morning, Little Alpesh went for a walk in the park. It was a blustery, gustery day and cold enough to be winter already. Little Alpesh shuffled through the leaves and tried not to think of conkers. This wasn't easy because there were conker pods everywhere – he could hear them crunching under his feet and see them spread out over the grass beneath the trees, all split and spiky and sad-looking because the conkers inside had been taken away and were now on the end of some kid's string being bashed to bits.

'You know, I never thought of that,' said Little Alpesh to himself. 'Maybe conker contests are *cruel* to conkers.'

'Codswallop,' said a voice.

'Sorry?' said Little Alpesh.

'Codswallop,' said the same voice. 'Never heard such stuff and nonsense. You must be about as brainy as a banana if you think conker contests are cruel to conkers.'

Where was the voice coming from?

Little Alpesh stared upwards and downwards and from side to side — by now he'd had plenty of practice at this — yet he couldn't see anyone. He was the only person in the park that Sunday morning.

'Conkers *love* conker contests,' the voice came again. 'It's their only chance to conquer each other before they conkersequently conk out!'

And the voice laughed and laughed and laughed in a shrill, spooky cackle. Now how would you like to be laughed at, close up, by someone you couldn't even see? Little Alpesh was *terrified*. Could this person, whoever it was, be dodging quickly behind him whenever he turned round? This time Little Alpesh spun in a circle so fast he almost left his clothes back to front.

Still there was no one there!

'Hee, hee, hee!' giggled the voice. 'You're as dozy as a dog-biscuit if you think you can catch me that way. Just listen to me, young feller-me-lad. If you want to see me, shut your eyes tight.'

'Eh?' said Little Alpesh. 'How can I see you with my eyes tight shut?'

'Well, you're not having much luck when they're wide open, are you?'

'I suppose not.'

So Little Alpesh shut his eyes tight.

'Now blink them a bit,' said the voice, 'as if you were switching the world on and off.'

And that's what Little Alpesh did – blink-blink, blink-blink, blink-blink, blink-blink.

Suddenly, like a photo being developed in mid-air, the voice turned into an old man right there in front of Little Alpesh.

'You're a park-keeper!' he exclaimed. 'Or rather you look like a *sort of* park-keeper ...'

For the old man had a park-keeper's
uniform and a park-keeper's hat and a stick
with a point on the end that was very park-
keeperish. Yet what was it that made him
only a *sort of* park-keeper? Could it have been
his *wizardy* face?

'Pleased to meet you,' said Little Alpesh.'

15

The park-keeper smiled. 'And I'm pleased to meet you, Little Alpesh.'

'How do you know my name?'

'Oh, I picked it up somewhere. You'd be surprised what I can pick up with this stick of mine. For example, something else I've picked up is what you've been looking for all this time . . .'

'You mean . . .'

'It's here in my pocket. And you can have it, if you like, for your very own – provided you make me a promise.'

'What promise, mister?'

'That whatever happens to you during the rest of this conker season – *whatever* happens, mind – you won't get big-headed.'

'Me?' said Little Alpesh. 'Big-headed? Never!'

'Here you are, then.'

And the sort of park-keeper with the wizardy face handed over a little box – a plump, pink, posh little box of the kind you get from a jeweller's shop. But there wasn't a sparkling brooch inside or a glittery ring or a smart new wristwatch. When Little Alpesh opened it, he found —

'A conker!'

And he blinked with astonishment. Maybe it was the blink that did it because when he looked up there was nobody else there. He was on his own in the park again ... except now he had the conker.

'It must be,' whispered Little Alpesh. 'It's got to be ... it's dead certain sure to be —'

THE CONKER AS HARD AS A DIAMOND.

It was, too.

Chapter Two

Or was it?

The conker as hard as a diamond, I mean. After all, apart from its fancy box it didn't

look at all special. What was there here to make Little Alpesh big-headed, for goodness sake?

He took the conker out for a closer look.

'Glad it's already on a bootlace,' said Little Alpesh. 'That saves me a bit of trouble. Surely this isn't *really* the conker as hard as a diamond?'

He tapped it: tap-tap. It sounded like an ordinary conker.

He sniffed it: sniff-sniff. It smelled like an ordinary conker.

He licked it: lick-lick. It tasted like an ordinary conker.

Yuk!

In fact this conker was just about as ordinary as it could possibly be. It lay there, in the palm of Little Alpesh's hand, all round and brown and conkery-looking just like a midget boxing-glove with its thumb missing. In other words, it was the same as all the other conkers you've ever come across.

'How can I become Conker Champion of the Universe with this?' wailed Little Alpesh. 'It'll bust straight away like all my conkers did last year.'

Sadly, he started for home. But he was a cheerful little chap, was Alpesh, and pretty soon he was whistling as he walked and twirling the conker on the end of its string so it flashed in the Sunday sunlight.

At the park gates he met some friends of his.

'Hello, Alpesh,' they said. 'See you've found the conker as hard as a diamond!'

'That's right,' laughed Little Alpesh. 'Better keep clear of it or it'll knock you into the middle of next week – maybe as far as Friday.'

'Great!' said the kids. 'We'd miss a whole week's school just about. See you, Alpesh.'

'See you,' called Alpesh.

And he twirled the conker harder than ever.

Now, just outside the park there happened to be an old tree — and when I say old I mean really, truly old. This tree was absolutely *historical*. For years and years and years it had been rained upon till it was completely soggy inside. Also the frost had got at it so the trunk was splintered and blotchy, and worst of all a couple of summers ago it had been struck by lightning during a terrific thunderstorm, making every branch black and powdery. Believe me, the tree was a mess. The only smart thing about it was the notice that had been put up by the Council. This said:

DANGER. KEEP OFF. THIS TREE IS AS DEAD AS A DOORKNOCKER AND SO WILL YOU BE IF IT FALLS ON YOUR BONCE.

Well, it said something like that, anyway.

'What a ponky old tree,' said Little Alpesh.

'About time the Council got rid of it, if you ask me.'

And still whistling, still twirling his conker, he walked past. Or nearly past. For it turned out that on one of its twirls Alpesh's conker *just* managed to brush against the tree. Very, very slightly, you understand.

It was hard enough, though. Because what

came next made Little Alpesh jump like a jiminy cricket.

Timber!

CRASH – CLONK – BONKETY – BONK!

'Wow!' yelped Little Alpesh.

He was lucky not to be as dead as a doorknocker because he was standing up to his knees in black, battered old tree. It was spread out all around him like a full-size Do-It-Yourself tree-struck-by-lightning kit, just out of its box. Alpesh held up the conker.

'Did you do that?' he asked.

The conker swung gently to and fro on its string.

'No,' said Little Alpesh. 'No ... you couldn't have.'

Just then –

Hee-Haw! Hee-Haw! Hee-Haw! Hee-Haw!

Everybody knows that sound. Either it's a seaside donkey having a temper-tantrum or it's the Police.

'Hello, officer,' said Little Alpesh.

The sergeant who got out of the Panda car was so gigantic and so hairy he looked like a gingery Santa Claus dressed up in a policeman's outfit.

'You all right, son?' he said.

'Fine,' said Little Alpesh. 'Er, I think it was my fault, sir. Reckon I was the one to blame – though I didn't do it on purpose, honestly.'

'Your fault? How come, son?'

'My conker.'

'What?'

'You see, it bashed against the tree just before it fell down ...'

'Your conker?'

'That's right. I was just kind of twirling it as I passed the tree and – what's so funny, sir?'

'Your conker?'

The policeman was laughing so much now that his whole face was like a huge gingery jelly wobbling up and down.

'Tell you what, son,' he spluttered. 'You know what that makes your conker, don't you?'

'No?'

'It makes it a *one-er*! You'd better get home quick before I decide to take it into protective custody!'

'You mean put it in prison, sir?'

'Certainly, son. Powerful conker like that

25

shouldn't be out on the loose. Threat to public order, that there conker is.'

As Little Alpesh hurried off he could hear the policeman still giggling madly.

Now, just a bit further on towards where Alpesh lived there happened to be a tumbledown house – and when I say tumbledown I mean really, truly tumbledown. The slates were falling off the roof, the windows were boarded up and on the front door was that chalk-mark which tells you the electricity people have switched off all the power. This house was in a right state! The only neat and tidy thing about it was the notice that had been put up by the Council. This said:

DANGER. KEEP OUT. THIS HOUSE IS AS DODGY AS A DINGBAT AND SO WILL YOU BE IF YOU ARE UNDER IT WHEN IT COLLAPSES.

Well, that was more or less what it said.

'What a grotty house,' said Little Alpesh. 'Really spoils the view it does. About time the Council pulled it down.' And he walked past, whistling, and twirling his conker. Or nearly walked past, rather. This time the conker just *grazed* the house ...

CRASH – BANG – WALLOP and TINKLE-TINKLE, too!

Little Alpesh felt as dodgy as a dingbat standing there waist-high in slates and plaster and bricks and broken glass. He

hadn't got a mark on him, though, and neither had the conker. It swayed gently to and fro as he held it up.

'Did you do that?' he asked. 'No ... no. You couldn't ... you couldn't possibly have.'

Hee-Haw! Hee-Haw! Hee-Haw! Hee-Haw!

Yes, it was the same sergeant with the same gingeriness.

'Son,' he said anxiously. 'Son – you all right?'

'Fine,' said Little Alpesh. 'But I'd better own up, sir. It was an accident, you see, but my conker –'

'Your conker?'

'It just grazed against the house and –'

Too late. Already the policeman was snorting and sneezing with laughter fit to bust his boots.

'What a right caution you are, son,' he chortled. 'That there conker of yours is enough to cause a breach of the peace, it is. I ought to run it in for obstruction, malicious damage and being an accessory before, after and during the fracas! There's only one word for your conker, son.'

'Yes, sir?'

'It's a *two-er*! Kindly move along at once before I set up a road-block all round it. Good-bye, son.'

Now, I don't want to tell you the next bit of the story. I just can't see you believing it at all. Unfortunately, it *is* what happened next so I've got to go on. Take a deep breath, then. Ready?

Right on the corner of the street where Little Alpesh lived there was this ... this ... MULTI-STOREYED CAR PARK.

It was enormous.

It was brand new.

It was what everybody needed.

Also it was a big mistake: it had been built back to front, you see, because the workmen had started with their plans upside-down. So

right in front of it stood yet another notice that had been put up by the Council. This said:

DANGER. KEEP AWAY. THIS MULTI-STOREYED CAR PARK IS AS DAFT AS A DICKORY-DOCK AND SO WILL YOU BE IF YOU ARE INSIDE WHEN WE DUFF IT UP.

Well, that's the kind of thing it said, anyhow.

'What a mingy multi-storeyed car park,' said Little Alpesh. 'Fancy building it back to front! Drivers wouldn't know if they were coming or going. About time the Council demolished it, in my opinion.'

And he walked past it — very nearly.

A whistle.

A twirl.

A nudge from the conker and . . .

KAPOW – WOW – WOW – WOW – WOW!

Little Alpesh felt as daft as a dickory-dock standing there up to his neck in a duffed-up multi-storeyed car park. When he'd clambered free, though, he discovered once again that he hadn't got a single scratch. Nor had the conker.

Hee-Haw! Hee-Haw! Hee-Haw! Hee-Haw!

'Don't tell me, son. Don't tell me. That aforementioned conker like what is in your possession is a now a *three-er!*'

But as the giant, gingery sergeant gazed

over acre after acre of wreckage his laughter slowly died away. Little Alpesh didn't like the new look on his face one little bit.

'Just a minute, son,' the sergeant said. 'Let's be having a look at that there catastrophe of a conker ...'

Too late.

Already Little Alpesh was round the corner, running licketysplit. I'm not surprised,

32

are you? Wouldn't you be in a hurry to get home if it had just been proved that you really, truly owned THE CONKER AS HARD AS A DIAMOND?

Chapter Three

Little Alpesh was worried.

If you'd seen the way he looked now you wouldn't have recognized him, I bet. Of course, he still had the wide-awake eyes and the jet-black hair but what was missing was his big, matey grin. Every time he thought about the conker as hard as a diamond he wanted to boo-hoo as if he were a baby.

'Why did you give it to me?' he wailed. 'Yes, you — the park-keeper with the wizardy face, I mean. What was it you said? I could have the conker for my very own provided I didn't get big-headed about it? How can I get big-headed about a conker that's so strong it's like having a bomb on a bit of string? What will it bash up next, I wonder?

34

The Town Hall? The Houses of Parliament?
Buckingham Palace?'

Little Alpesh longed to tell someone all
about it but who could he trust? His Mum
and Dad were still in Pakistan visiting his
grandparents and his uncles and aunts. They
wouldn't be back for weeks yet. The only
person left was his Big Sister Sameena and
she might tease him.

Not this time, though.

'The old tree,' she gasped. 'The empty

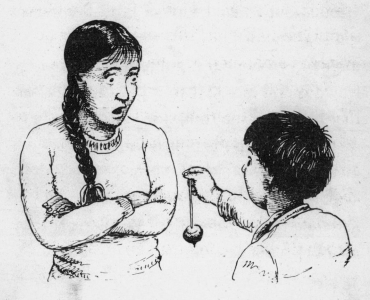

house? And then the multi-storeyed car park? You knocked them all down?'

'Not me,' protested Little Alpesh. 'It was my conker. I just happened to be holding it at the time.'

'Oh yes?' sniffed Big Sister Sameena. 'Oh yes?'

Little Alpesh sighed. If his own sister didn't believe him then who would? And suppose that policeman – the huge, gingery-whiskered sergeant who drove the Panda car – found out where he lived? Probably he was out looking for Little Alpesh at this very moment, with a huge, gingery-whiskered frown on his face that told you clear as clear that he hoped the conker would come along quietly and help the police with their inquiries.

But what if the conker accidentally flattened the police station? Wouldn't that count as resisting arrest?

'I've got to get shot of this conker,' Little Alpesh groaned.

'Could've told you that,' said Big Sister Sameena. 'How are you going to do it?'

'Down the loo?'

'What, and then pull the chain? With that conker you'll end up flooding the street, more than likely.'

'Burn it?'

'Oh great. Be like Firework Night, that would. Reckon your conker is explosive.'

'Okay, mastermind. What can I do, then?'

Sameena jerked a thumb at their back-yard.

'Dustbin,' she said. 'Take my word for it. It's bound to work. But you'd better be quick. The dustman's almost due.'

So Little Alpesh shoved the conker as hard as a diamond deep down into the bin amongst the tin cans, fish-bones and tea-leaves. He was only just in time.

'What are you chucking away, kid?' asked the dustman suspiciously.

'My conker.'

'That all? Reckon we can handle that okay – got the very latest mechanical garbage-gobbler out there, we have. It's brand new, super-de-luxe and they say it chews up just about *anything*.'

'See what I mean?' said Sameena.

'Want to come and watch?' the dustman invited.

'Thanks,' said Little Alpesh.

Of course, really it was the last thing he wanted to do. He knew that he'd be saying good-bye to his one and only chance of being Conker Champion of the Universe ...

Garbage-gobble, garbage-gobble, garbage-gobble went the dustman's garbage-gobbler. Little Alpesh, Sameena and the dustman stood at the back with the empty dustbin and watched the rubbish being chewed up in the machine. Suddenly — FIZZ-BOING!

'What's that?' said the dustman.

Garbage-gobble, Fizz-Boing! Garbage-gobble, Fizz-Boing! Garbage-gobble, Fizz-Boing! went the machine.

'There it is again,' said the dustman. 'That's not right. What's a Fizz-Boing doing in my garbage-gobbler? And where's all the smoke coming from?'

'I can see flames, too,' said Little Alpesh.

'Your garbage-gobbler doesn't look brand new and super-de-luxe now,' said Sameena.

'Oh crikey!' shrieked the dustman. 'Help! Call Fire, Police and Ambulance, someone!'

'I'll do it,' said Sameena.

But before she could move, the garbage-gobbler made a sudden rude noise halfway between a burp and a hiccup and something bounced out of the flap at the back. It rolled over the pavement towards Little Alpesh.

'It's my conker,' said Little Alpesh.

'Pick it up quick, kid,' the dustman groaned. 'Obviously it doesn't fancy being a roasted chestnut. Can't say I blame it. I don't fancy taking a roasted garbage-gobbler back to the depot, either.'

Little Alpesh stared in horror at the conker cupped in his hand. Already it was a *four-er* and he hadn't even played a contest yet! So far, all it had brought him was trouble. And was that a Hee-Haw! Hee-Haw! Hee-Haw! he could hear?

'Hey, where are you off to?' exclaimed the dustman.

'What's the hurry, Alpesh?' Sameena called.

But Little Alpesh had got an idea. He was running full pelt, I can tell you — huff-and-puff, huff-and-puff, huff-and-puff — alongside the wreck of the multi-storeyed car park — huff-and-puff, huff-and-puff, huff-and-puff — past what was left of the house and left of the tree — huff-and-puff, huff-and-puff, huff-and-puff — between the park gates, under the conker trees and down as far as the river. He didn't stop till he got to the busiest part of the waterfront.

'Perishin' huff and perishin' puff,' gasped Little Alpesh.

As soon as he'd got his breath back, he stared up and up and up through the cranes and the hoists and the loading gear that hovere   above the deck of a vast, gleaming, ready-to-sail cargo boat.

'Australia?' said Little Alpesh. 'Iceland? South America? I don't care which. You're just what I need!' And with all his strength he hurled the conker away cricket-style, so it looped through the air right into the cargo boat's main funnel.

'Good riddance,' Little Alpesh yelled as he walked away.

Behind him the boat's hooter said its good-bye: parp-parp!

'Phew!' said Little Alpesh.

But before he could get his big, matey grin back on his face he heard ... a grinding noise. A gravelly, glug-glug, gurgling noise.

'Abandon ship!' came a faint shout.

Little Alpesh stood absolutely still.

'It can't be ...' he whispered.

Yet it was. Echoing along the waterfront came the sound of a vast, gleaming, ready-

to-sail cargo boat slowly kerplunking to the
bottom of the river.

'I don't believe it,' shrieked Little Alpesh.
'Already it's a *five-er* and it's never bumped
another conker!'

'If you say so, son,' came a giant, gingery
voice. 'Thanks to you, we've now got a bit

43

of a rescue job on our hands. But once we've saved that conker of yours, not to mention the entire contents and crew of that there rapidly sinking vessel, you'd better come along with me to the police station to answer a few questions.'

Oh dear. The sergeant with the Panda car had caught up with Little Alpesh at last. His adventures with the conker as hard as a diamond were well and truly over.

At least, I think they were.

Chapter Four

The conker as hard as a diamond was now in gaol.

Just think of it: four whitewashed walls like a tall bathroom without any bathroom tiles; one high-up window with bars as thick as a tiger's tail; one steel door locked so tight not even a burglar the size of a flea could get in or out.

Oh yes – in the corner there was a bunk as well. On this lay the conker. The sunlight, as it streamed through the iron bars of the window, glinted on its shiny skin. Also it glinted on a tear running down Little Alpesh's cheek. It was visiting time and he'd come to prepare the conker for its trial.

'You can't blame me,' said Little Alpesh. 'It was all your own fault.'

The conker said nothing.

'I mean, you've been asking for trouble right from the start. Why did you have to bash up everything that got in your way? There's no sense to it. And how d'you reckon my Mum and Dad will feel when they arrive home from Pakistan? They've probably told the rest of the family how well they're doing in England – and when they get back they'll find they're the parents of a kid who owns a criminal conker. They'll be so ashamed! What do you say to that?'

Not a word from the conker.

'You'll be shut away for years and years and years, I shouldn't wonder. Already they've taken away your bootlace so you can't batter this place down. Worst of all, I haven't even had a match with you yet. What's the point of owning a conker as hard as a diamond if you don't even have a single conker fight?'

Still there wasn't a peep from the conker. Was it stone-deaf, do you think?

Suddenly there was a rattle at the steel door, followed by the sound of a key as it turned in a lock, the scrape of several bolts being drawn back, the clink of an unravelling chain and the grinding noise of a portcullis –

which is a kind of iron grid – as it lifted upwards. The police weren't taking any chances with the conker as hard as a diamond.

'On your feet, son,' snapped the sergeant with the ginger beard. 'Visiting time is over. His Lordship the Judge wants to see that conker straightaway. Also he wants a word with *you*. Just hold on a tick while I get out my handcuffs.'

'Handcuffs?' said Little Alpesh. 'But I'm not a prisoner, sir. I'm a witness.'

'I know that, son. The handcuffs aren't for you. They're for the conker.'

'The conker? How can you handcuff a conker?'

The sergeant smiled grimly.

'Son, I didn't say it would be easy. But this here horror of a horse-chestnut has got to be overpowered before I can take it into court.'

'Good luck,' said Little Alpesh.

Half an hour later the conker finally hung from the sergeant's left wrist after he'd screwed up the handcuffs as tight as they could get. Even so, the sergeant didn't feel safe and I don't blame him. Would you like to be shackled to a conker so magic it could knock down a multi-storeyed car park and sink a cargo boat? You would? Wait and see what happens, then.

'Hurry up,' the sergeant grumbled. 'His

49

Lordship the Judge is waiting. Wouldn't be surprised if he doesn't lock up this bleep-bleep, blankety-blank conker and throw away the key. By the time it gets out of gaol it'll be so shrivelled up it'll be smaller than a salted peanut – and serve it right.'

His Lordship the Judge wasn't the only one who was waiting. The courtroom was packed out. Almost everyone Little Alpesh knew was there. Next to Big Sister Sameena, for example, sat his rich Uncle Vimesh – who'd shut up his shop especially, though it wasn't even early-closing day. Now Little Alpesh was sure it was serious. As he gazed round at his relatives and friends, at the policeman and court-helpers, at the reporters and at the visitors who were just plain nosey, he realized what it was they were so curious about.

THE CONKER AS HARD AS A DIAMOND.

I expect you know all about courtrooms

from films on television, but in case you don't here's what it was like:

There was the Dock (which is where the prisoner sits).

There was the Well-of-the-Court (which is where the helpers sit).

There was the Public Gallery (which is where the watchers sit).

There was the Bench (which is where his Lordship the Judge sits in his posh robe and crinkly wig).

And there was the Witness Box ... which is where Little Alpesh sat.

His Lordship the Judge rapped on his desk with a small wooden hammer and the hubbub in the courtroom died down at once.

'Sergeant, be good enough to lift up the prisoner so we can all see it. Now then, first witness, what is your name?'

'Little Alpesh, my Lord.'

'And is it true, Little Alpesh, that the

Accused – this conker – belongs to you?
Was it really given to you by a sort of park-
keeper with a wizardy face?'

'Yes,' whispered Little Alpesh. 'He said I
could have it for my very own – provided I
promised that whatever happened I didn't
get big-headed.'

'Big-headed?' the Judge exclaimed. 'You
must be pin-headed to be the owner of a

conker as dangerous as this. Do you admit that so far it has brought about the public clobberation of an old tree, a derelict house, a multi-storeyed car park built back to front, a brand-new council garbage-gobbler and a vast, gleaming, ready-to-sail cargo boat?'

'Yes, my Lord. I'm ever so sorry.'

'It's not enough to be sorry, Little Alpesh. You can't nip round to all the things your conker has destroyed and kiss them better, you know. Think yourself lucky nobody was actually hurt. Normally I'd make the prisoner pay for all the damage that's been caused, but since the conker doesn't get any pocket-money I'll have to put it in prison *forever*. Sergeant, hold the prisoner steady, please, while I pass sentence upon it ... I said keep it still, sergeant. Why are you swinging it backwards and forwards?'

'I'm not, your Lordship,' gulped the sergeant. 'It seems to be swinging itself.'

Which is exactly what was happening, of course. To and fro, to and fro, swung the conker as hard as a diamond. A hush fell over the courtroom as everyone gaped at it.

To and fro, to and fro.

At the end of one of its swings, the conker just managed to *brush* against the prisoner's dock.

CRASH – CLONK – BONKETY – BONK!

Then the conker bounced out of the

sergeant's handcuffs, bib-bobbed across the courtroom and just *grazed* the Judge's bench.

CLATTER-BANG!

From here, the conker rolled over the floor until it just *touched* the Public Gallery.

KAPOW!

What an amazing sight ... in less than the time it takes to dial 999 the whole courtroom was a shambles. Once again, Little Alpesh just couldn't believe it. All round him was smashed-up furniture, a jumble of books and documents, and arms and legs waving in the air. Honestly, he felt so ashamed of his conker he was ready to cry his eyes out. But how could he – in front of all these grown-ups and Uncle Vimesh and Big Sister Sameena? To keep the tears away he blinked.

Blink-blink. Blink-blink. Blink-blink. Blink-blink.

Suddenly ...

Who was that laughing? Where had Little Alpesh heard that shrill, spooky cackle before? Could it be ...

'Yes,' said a voice. 'It's me with the wizardy face again.'

There, smack in the middle of the chaos, was an old man who had a park-keeper's uniform, a park-keeper's hat and a stick with a point on the end that was very park-keeperish. Where had he come from? You could see straight away that the Judge wasn't pleased to see him. After all, how happy would you be if your robe was dusty and torn, your wig was skew-whiff, your courtroom was totally wrecked and then you were lumbered with a surprise witness?

'What do you want?' his Lordship snarled.

The old man smiled a blustery, gustery, park-keeperish smile.

'First,' he said, 'I'm here to pay for all the

damage caused by the conker as hard as a diamond – every last penny of it. That's only fair since I gave the thing to Little Alpesh in the first place. Second, I'm here to invite you to the Contest.'

'The Contest?' snapped the Judge. 'What Contest?'

'At this time of the year there's only one Contest worth mentioning,' said the old man.

'I'm talking about ... THE CONKER
CHAMPIONSHIP OF THE UNIVERSE.'

'THE CONKER CHAMPIONSHIP OF THE
UNIVERSE?' gasped Little Alpesh.

'Exactly. It'll be the greatest Contest of its
kind that's ever been staged. Already I've
had letters from the Queen and the Prime
Minister and the Archbishop of Canterbury
begging me for tickets. Naturally, I'll do
them a favour if I possibly can. But, apart
from his Lordship, the most important person
there could be *you*, Little Alpesh.'

'Me?'

'You and the conker as hard as a diamond.'

'We'll ... we'll be taking part, you mean?'

'Taking part? Little Alpesh, provided you
don't get big-headed, you might even turn
out to be the *winner*. What do you say to
that?'

Well, if you were Little Alpesh what
would you have said? I'll bet your voice

would've echoed round the courtroom just as loud and just as long as his did.

'YIPPEEEEEEEEEEEEEE!!!'

Chapter Five

Are you ready for THE CONKER
CHAMPIONSHIP OF THE UNIVERSE to begin?

Little Alpesh was. His eyes were more
wide-awake than ever, he'd brushed his jet-
black hair till it shone – and for all I know
he'd even given a special polish to his big,
matey grin. Well, wouldn't you if you were
the proud owner of THE CONKER AS HARD
AS A DIAMOND? Every so often Little Alpesh
would open up the plump, pink, posh little
box of the kind you get from a jeweller's
shop and take a peek inside, just in case. And
there it still was – all round and brown and
conkery-looking and more than ever like a
midget boxing-glove with its thumb missing.

But it *wasn't* an ordinary conker, was it? This conker was a *six-er* before it had even had its first contest! No wonder Little Alpesh was happy.

'Yippee!' he yelled for the hundredth time. 'I'm going to be Conker Champion of the Universe!'

'You be careful,' warned his Big Sister Sameena. 'Things could still go wrong, you know.'

'How come?'

'Remember what that old bloke with the wizardy face said? He was giving you the conker only if you promised that whatever happens to you during the rest of this conker season – what ever happens, mind – *you won't get big-headed.*'

'Okay, okay, okay,' said Little Alpesh. 'You needn't keep on about it. I won't forget old wizardy-bonce.'

And he took out the box for yet another

quick check. Yes, the conker as hard as a diamond was still snug as ever.

'Just think of it,' whispered Little Alpesh. 'Conker Champion of the Universe ...'

Big Sister Sameena sighed.

Well, be honest. Aren't you a bit worried? Could it be that the head of Little Alpesh was swelling up just a fraction? Even if it was, can you really blame him? Over the entire world, remember, kids who'd never even heard of conkers before were now training hard – in Iceland, in Africa, in China, in every country you can name. You see, thanks to the Championship, conker playing had become more popular than swimming, football, tennis, horse-riding, gymnastics, ice-skating, darts or snooker, all rolled into one. It was the most exciting sport on earth. Lorries, ships and aeroplanes hustled and bustled everywhere with cargoes of conkers for places where conker trees didn't grow. Just imagine millions and millions of kids all busy giving their favourite conker special treatment ... such as soaking in vinegar, or baking hard in the oven or freezing solid in the fridge!

Little Alpesh didn't have to do any of this, of course. For how can you improve on a conker that's already as hard as a diamond?

Other kids, too, had to battle through the preliminary heats, a whole series of knock-out contests, to prove that their conker and their conkership were good enough to win them a place in the Final. Yet Little Alpesh and his world-famous conker were already *in* the Final — everybody agreed that *they* were good enough. So it's not surprising he felt ever so slightly swanky. This bothered Big Sister Sameena a lot.

'Shouldn't you be out practising?' she asked.

'Practising?' said Little Alpesh. 'How can I practise? Only a diamond as big as my conker would be hard enough for me to practise with. Where would I get a jewel as enormous as that? Not even the Queen has got a diamond that size. Come to think of it, after I've won the Conker Championship of the Universe I might give the Queen my conker as a present. She can wear it in her crown.'

64

'You're swanking again,' said Big Sister Sameena.

'No, I'm not. I'm just confident, that's all. Tell me which kid and which conker can possibly beat me.'

'*You*, Alpesh. And the conker as hard as a diamond.'

'Eh?'

'You'll end up beating yourself if you get big-headed.'

'I wouldn't be such a wally,' said Little Alpesh.

'Wouldn't you?'

Big Sister Sameena wasn't so sure.

She needn't have worried, though, because that very night on the six o'clock news came a report that frightened Little Alpesh so much he had goosepimples on top of his goosepimples.

Hyram Drongo, the richest kid in America, had decided to enter for the Conker Championship of the Universe.

'Hyram Drongo?' Little Alpesh gasped. 'He's so rich he has to use a calculator to keep track of his pocket-money. Presidents and Film Stars and other Top People send him birthday presents just to stay friendly with him — sometimes when it's not even his birthday.'

'What difference does it make how rich he is?' Sameena asked. 'He'll only be as good as his conker.'

'Don't you understand?' groaned Little Alpesh. 'He can *buy* a super-duper conker or even *invent* a super-duper conker — a person as stinking rich as he is can always rely on someone to get him what he wants.'

Little Alpesh was quite right to be scared. That night, on the eight o'clock news, it was reported that every single Drongo dollar was being risked to make sure Hyram Drongo became Conker Champion of the Universe.

Drongo farms, Drongo forests and Drongo factories – not to mention the Drongo computer-laboratories and the Drongo space-research programme – were all working on the same project. A major breakthrough in conkerology was expected any hour.

On the ten o'clock news came the worst report of all. Little Alpesh had been allowed to stay up late so he could hear it.

Afterwards he wished he hadn't.

'Hyram Drongo has got his conker,' said the newsreader. 'It's a conker so stunning and so secret that a special underground conker shelter has been built to keep it safe till the day of the Contest.'

'See?' wailed Little Alpesh. 'See? I told you he'd come up with a conker as good as mine — maybe even better than mine.'

'At least you're not big-headed now,' Big Sister Sameena said.

Poor Little Alpesh hardly got a wink of sleep that night. He tossed and turned in his bed as if it had been stuffed with a million conkers, all of them belonging to Hyram Drongo. But there was worse to come. Next morning, as he was cleaning his teeth and listening to the radio, he heard another news bulletin:

'This is the eight o'clock news. Russia has

just announced its competitor for the Conker Championship of the Universe. Her name is Tanya Bottyoff — already famous as the only nine-year-old ever to win a world weightlifting title. The Russians have been forced to invent a special bootlace made of super-toughened steel to fit Miss Bottyoff's conker since she's snapped every other sort of conker string during practice. So far no details have been released of the Russian conker itself, which is said to be *the first of its kind.* At this very moment, under heavy guard, the conker is on display in Red Square, Moscow. Millions of Russians have already formed a queue many miles long and are filing past to pay their respects.'

When he heard all this Little Alpesh was so upset he almost swallowed his toothbrush. What chance had he got up against the might of Russia and the money of America even if he did have the conker as hard as a diamond on his side? He was only an ordinary kid, after all.

'It's hopeless,' he groaned. 'See, maybe we should give up right now.'

'What?' said Big Sister Sameena. 'Say that again.'

'Maybe we should give up right now.'

At this point I need a bit of assistance. There's no way for me to describe the look on Big Sister Sameena's face because words

70

just aren't wordy enough, especially my words. So kindly lend me your face for a moment. Stay where you are and don't move at all — except every part of you that's above your neck. Now, twist your mouth and cheeks and nose and eyebrows and ears, from your forehead to your chin, into the angriest — snarliest — most tantrum-like expression you possibly can. Be careful not to look in a mirror while you're doing it, though, because that could bring seven year's bad luck.

Is that the worst you can come up with? Good!

Now, relax.

The face you've just pulled is only about half as cross as the one Big Sister Sameena pulled when Little Alpesh said that he and the conker as hard as a diamond should give up even before the Contest had started. She scared Little Alpesh stiff. Really she did.

'Sorry, sorry, sorry,' he said hastily.

'I should think so, too. If you quit now then you'll be as dead as a doorknocker, as dodgy as a dingbat and as daft as a dickory-dock. What I'm trying to say is that I'd rather you were a *big-head* than a *quitter*.'

'Would you?'

'Of course, I would. So would anybody.'

'Okay,' sighed Little Alpesh. 'I'll go ahead then. Even if my conker does get duffed up good and proper. And even if Americans and Russians are playing conkers for the very first time in history just to win the Contest, which strikes me as being not blinkin' fair.'

Poor, grumpy Little Alpesh.

So this was the line-up then on Conker Eve — which is what everyone called the day before the Conker Championship of the Universe:

Hyram Drongo and his multi-millionairish conker.

Tanya Bottyoff and her superpower conker.

Little Alpesh and the conker as hard as a diamond.

Would you like me to tell you the winner? Okay, I will then ... soon.

Chapter Six

Hurry up!

You're just in time.

The day fixed for the Conker Championship of the Universe had come at last. Everyone, everywhere, who could get to a television set had been stuck in front of the screen for hours and hours, all breathless and fidgety and tingling from top to toe. As for the people in the actual stadium, they were even more excited. They'd won their tickets in a great, free raffle organized by the park-keeper with the wizardy face and they felt so special it was as if each of them had been knighted by King Arthur himself.

So why hadn't the Contest started?

*

'All this hanging about doesn't help,' grumbled Big Sister Sameena. 'It'll put Little Alpesh right off. Look at him down there on the conker pitch, Uncle Vimesh — it's obvious he's nervous. Good job Mum and Dad decided to stay in Pakistan and watch with the rest of the family. If they were here, he'd be even more jittery. Look at the way he's blinking.'

Blink-blink, blink-blink, blink-blink.

Suddenly ...

Taran-tara! Taran-tara!

'It's *him*,' Big Sister Sameena exclaimed.

She meant the old man, of course. There he was — kitted out with a park-keeper's uniform, a park-keeper's hat and a stick with a point on the end that was very park-keeperish. Look a bit more closely, though. Didn't he make you think of a *special* kind of park ... a magic park where the roundabouts push themselves, the slides have an escalator instead of steps and you can loop-the-loop on the swings without falling off? And how was it that every conker fan in the North, South, East and West of the world was able to hear him when there wasn't a single microphone to pick up his voice?

'Welcome!' he said. 'My name is Mr Wizardy-Sir and today is the most important day in the history of conkers. For the first time ever we are here to decide THE CONKER CHAMPIONSHIP OF THE UNIVERSE. The rules are very simple: no *wheelies*, no *heelies* and no *snicker-snacker*. In this Contest only one thing counts — clunk, click and clobber-the-conker! Does everyone understand? And does everyone agree?'

Hyram Drongo, with his multi-millionairish conker, nodded. Tanya Bottyoff, with her superpower conker, nodded. And holding on tight to the conker as hard as a diamond, Little Alpesh nodded. Mr Wizardy-Sir tilted back his head and looked up and up.

'Do you understand and agree?' he asked.

Was it the rest of the Universe he was talking to? Every boy and girl who was watching crossed fingers, hoping the sky would nod, too.

And perhaps it did. At any rate, Mr Wizardy-Sir smiled.

'Then we can begin,' he said. 'I've checked the conkers and they are all perfectly fair – a

bit *odd*, maybe, but still fair. Also I've tossed
a conker to find out the order of play. So if
everyone's ready we'll begin with Round
One —'

'Taran-tara! Taran-tara!

'— which is between Hyram Drongo and
Little Alpesh.'

At this point there was so much clapping
and cheering and stamping it's a wonder the
world didn't wobble. But it went quiet at
once when Mr Wizardy-Sir lifted his stick.

'On my right, the conker as hard as a
diamond,' he announced. 'And on my left ...
the *Nuclear Rubber Bonker Conker*!'

'The Nuclear Rubber Bonker Conker?'
gasped Big Sister Sameena. 'Does that
mean ...'

'It does,' groaned Uncle Vimesh. 'Just look
at Hyram warming it up.'

Do you remember me telling you that
Little Alpesh had wide-awake eyes, jet-back

hair and a grin on his face so big and friendly that you felt like his best mate the instant you met him? Well, Hyram Drongo was the exact opposite. He had piggy-eyes, Goldilocks-hair and a scowl on his face as if you were his worst enemy. In fact, he was just as nasty-looking as his conker.

With one hand, Hyram held up a brass doorknob on the end of a piece of string. With the other, he swung the Nuclear Rubber Bonker Conker. Just once.

Dobba-dobba-dobba-dobba-dobba-dobba-dobba-dobba-dobba-dobba!

'It's incredible!' Sameena exclaimed. 'It's a million hits rolled into one – see? The doorknob's splitting in half!'

If this was just a practice, what chance had Little Alpesh in the real fight? Not much, everyone thought. All over the world necks craned forward and eyes bulged to get the best possible view. The silence was so huge you could've heard a ladybird cough.

Little Alpesh lifted his conker to take the first blow.

Hyram Drongo sniggered and lifted his conker to give the first strike.

Dobba-dobba-dobba-dobba-dobba-dobba-dobba-dobba-dobba-dobba!

'It's even more incredible,' whispered Big Sister Sameena. 'Hyram's conker has –'

Dobba-dobba-dobba-dobba-dobba-dobba-dobba-dobba-dobba-dobba!

'– completely –'

Dobba-dobba-dobba-dobba-dobba-dobba-dobba-dobba-dobba-dobba!

'vanished!'

Yes, like a piece of used-up soap, the Nuclear Rubber Bonker Conker had disappeared. All Hyram had in his hand was a piece of string.

'The conker as hard as a diamond is the winner ...'

At these words from Mr Wizardy-Sir there was a pandemonium of yelling and whistling, and hip-hip-hooraying. Everyone in the world who happened to be wearing a hearing-aid hastily switched it off.

'Oh dear,' sighed Big Sister Sameena. 'Please don't go all swanky like that, Little Alpesh – patting yourself on the back and blowing kisses and stuff. Can't you see Mr Wizardy-Sir doesn't like it?'

'... *is the winner of Round One*,' Mr Wizardy-Sir went on. 'Now for Round Two,

which is between Little Alpesh and Tanya
Bottyoff.'

Taran-tara! Taran-tara!

'On my right, the conker as hard as a
diamond and on my left ... *the Hairy Octo-
Conker!*'

'The Hairy Octo-Conker?' Big Sister
Sameena gasped. 'It's *horrible*, Uncle Vimesh –
just look at the way Tanya is combing its
tentacles with that garden fork. Eek! I can't
bear to look.'

'It's even uglier than she is,' said Uncle
Vimesh.

This was true. Tanya Bottyoff had eyes no
bigger than gnat-bites, Rumpelstiltskin-hair
and a mouth like a shark wishing you
good-bye. But the Hairy Octo-Conker was
even worse. For her warm-up Tanya held out
a cannonball on the end of a chain. Instantly
the tentacles stretched towards it.

Slurp-slurp-slurp-slurp-slurp-slurp!

The dreadful noise of the Hairy Octo-Conker as it sucked the cannonball smaller and smaller and smaller made half the world feel sick (the other half had shut their eyes and stuffed up their ears). Soon only the chain was left.

Trembling, not swanking at all any more, Little Alpesh raised the conker as hard as a diamond. It was so quiet you could've heard a spider sniff.

The tentacles of the Hairy Octo-Conker began to twitch, began to reach ... Then –

Pruls-pruls-pruls-pruls-pruls-pruls!

'It's gone into reverse!' exclaimed Big Sister Sameena. 'Can you see the tentacles shrivelling up, Uncle Vimesh? The Hairy Octo-Conker is going bald –'

Pruls-pruls-pruls-pruls-pruls-pruls!

'– and now there's no conker at all, just a dangly chain!'

'The conker as hard as a diamond is the winner ...'

Mr Wizardy-Sir's voice could only just be heard above a din so loud that deep-sea divers on the far side of the world quickly came back to the surface to find out what was wrong. You could just hear the voice of Little Alpesh, too.

'That's it! I've done it! I'm Conker Champion of the Universe! Who cares about soppy Hyram Drongo and dippy Tanya

Bottyoff? Who's bothered about the Hairy Octo-Conker and the Nuclear Rubber Conker? I've duffed them both up! Nyur-nyur-nyur!'

'Don't show off, Little Alpesh,' begged Big Sister Sameena. 'Otherwise —'

'Look at me, fans!' Little Alpesh boasted.

'I'm the greatest — the very greatest! I'm Conker Champion of the Universe!'

'No you're not,' said Mr Wizardy-Sir.

'Sorry?'

'That was Round Two, Little Alpesh.'

'Round Two? But ...'

'Round Three is still to come.'

With his stick, Mr Wizardy-Sir pointed.

Never before have so many people stared up at the sky at once. World-wide, people left their television sets to go to the window or climb on the roof. All the earth seemed to be saying: LOOK!

At first it was a speck, no more.

Then it became a blob.

After this it grew as big as a pumpkin — a Hallowe'en pumpkin with lights shining out of it. Or maybe we should call it a gigantic Hallowe'en conker because by the time this horse-chestnutty space-craft had landed in the stadium it was the size and

shape of the biggest circus tent you've
ever seen.

'Oh, Alpesh,' groaned Big Sister Sameena.

The door of the space-ship slid open. Out
stepped a creature who looked a bit like a
tortoise and a bit like a robot but most of all
like a baby. It still wore a nappy, you see.
That's how young it was. You could tell

straight away that it was an infant-alien — a friendly, giggly creature from the far side of the stars.

'Are you ... are you from three million light-years away?' asked Little Alpesh.

It was Mr Wizardy-Sir who answered.

'More than that, Little Alpesh. From umpteen million light-years away, to be exact. It's obvious, isn't it, that you can't have a Conker Championship of the *Universe* if it's only earth-people who enter? Here we have THE CONKER FROM OUTER SPACE. Of course, that doesn't necessarily make it better than *your* conker. What a magnificent Contest it would have been, young-feller-me-lad, if you hadn't let yourself get big-headed. Because you know what's going to happen next, don't you?'

'Yes,' whispered Little Alpesh.

'And you agree I gave you fair warning right from the start?'

'Yes.'

'So let's get it over with, shall we?'

Poor, poor Little Alpesh. Everyone in the world knew what was going to happen next. Maybe everyone in the Universe knew it, too. So perhaps everyone alive saw how *brave* he was because he twisted his face into the biggest, perkiest smile he could manage. Even Big Sister Sameena was proud of him.

'Mr Wizardy-Sir?' he asked.

'Yes, Little Alpesh?'

'Can I have the first bash, please? I want to make it a really good one.'

'Certainly,' said Mr Wizardy-Sir.

Well, it's a wonder the infant-alien's nappy didn't fall down from the shock of what happened next.

First, Little Alpesh took a long, hard look at the ghostly, shimmering CONKER FROM OUTER SPACE. Second, he lined up the string and got his fingers and thumbs into exactly

the right position. Third, with a superb
whiplash action, he let fly.

CRACK!

Instantly, the conker as hard as a diamond
split into umpteen million pieces each as light
as a year.

But guess who was first to congratulate
the winner and shake him by his strange,
spindly hand? And who led the hip-hip-

hoorays as the space-ship took off and soared away into the sky? Was it the Queen or the Prime Minister or the Archbishop of Canterbury?

No.

Was it Mr Wizardy-Sir or his Lordship the Judge or the sergeant with the gingery whiskers?

No.

Was it Uncle Vimesh or Big Sister Sameena?

No.

Was it ... yes! You've guessed it. It was the best sport of all: Little Alpesh.

Mind you, as soon as the space-ship was out of sight people couldn't help noticing the way Little Alpesh started staring upwards and downwards and from side to side as if he were looking for something. And another thing they couldn't help noticing was the way his eyes went blink-blink, blink-blink,

blink-blink, blink-blink. Could he possibly have been getting in some practice?

I reckon Little Alpesh will find the conker as hard as a diamond again next year, don't you?

Unless, of course, you find it first.

Good-bye.

BRIGHT-EYE
Alison Morgan

Amanda lives on a farm deep in the Welsh countryside. When her father brings home a wild duck's egg he has saved, Amada is determined to find a way of hatching it out. How wonderful if a beautiful fluffy duckling were to hatch out and become her own special pet! But things do not work out in quite the way she expects.

MR MAJEIKA
Humphrey Carpenter

The new teacher at St Barty's makes his first appearance in a very unusual way. And of course, as everyone is to find out, he's no ordinary teacher at all, however hard he may try to be. This is bad news for Hamish Bigmore, the class nuisance, who's been getting his own way for far too long.

THE PERFECT HAMBURGER
Alexander McCall Smith

If only Joe could remember exactly what he had thrown so haphazardly into the mixing bowl, he knew that his perfect hamburger could revive his friend's ailing business.

PROFESSOR BRANESTAWM'S MOUSE WAR
and
PROFESSOR BRANESTAWM'S BUILDING BUST-UP

Norman Hunter

Two more peculiar inventions by the hilarious Professor Branestawm. In the first, the Professor invents a house-building machine, and in the second he invents a cat-shaped balloon to rid Great Pagwell of its mice problem.

THE THREE AND MANY WISHES
OF JASON REID

Hazel Hutchins

Eleven-year-old Jason is a very good thinker. So when Quicksilver (no more than eighteen inches high) grants him three wishes, he's extremely wary. After all, in fairy tales, this kind of thing always leads to disaster. So Jason is absolutely determined to get *his* wishes right. But it's not that easy, and he lands himself and his friends in all sorts of terrible but funny scrapes!

MR BERRY'S ICE-CREAM PARLOUR

Jennifer Zabel

It is thrilling enough to have a lodger in the house — after all, not even Andrew Brimblecombe has a lodger — but Carl is over the moon when he discovers that Mr Berry plans to open an ice-cream parlour.